CONTENTS

LACH Y'RUSHALAYIM

Music: E Rubinstein
Lyrics: A Etinger
Piano Arr: E. Kalendar

5

or cha - dash ya - ir _____ b' - li -

bé - nu b' - li - bé - nu rak shir e - chad ka -

yam _____ lach Y' - ru - sha - la - yim _

bén yar - dén va - yam _____

Lach Y'-ru-sha-la-yim bén cho-mot ha-ir	לָךְ יְרוּשָׁלַיִם בֵּין חוֹמוֹת הָעִיר
Lach Y'-ru-sha-la-yim or cha-dash ya-ir	לָךְ יְרוּשָׁלַיִם אוֹר חָדָשׁ יָאִיר
Refrain	פזמון
B'-li-bé-nu rak shir e-chad ka-yam	בְּלִבֵּנוּ רַק שִׁיר אֶחָד קַיָּם
Lach Y'-ru-sha-la-yim bén Yar-dén va-yam	לָךְ יְרוּשָׁלַיִם בֵּין יַרְדֵּן וָיָם
Lach Y'-ru-sha-la-yim lach k'-du-mim va-hod	לָךְ יְרוּשָׁלַיִם לָךְ קְדוּמִים וָהוֹד
Lach y'-ru-sha-la-yim lach ra-zim va-sod *Refrain*	לָךְ יְרוּשָׁלַיִם לָךְ רָזִים וָסוֹד פזמון
Lach Y'-ru-sha-la-yim shir ni-sa ta-mid	לָךְ יְרוּשָׁלַיִם שִׁיר נִישָׂא תָּמִיד
Lach Y'-ru-sha-la-yim ir mig-dal Da-vid *Refrain*	לָךְ יְרוּשָׁלַיִם עִיר מִגְדַּל דָּוִד פזמון

For you, O Jerusalem, fortress of David, let a new light shine. In our hearts
there exists but one song, a song dedicated to you.

OSE SHALOM

Music: N. Hirsh
Text: Liturgy
Piano Arr: E. Kalendar

8

ya -a -se sha-lom   ya -a - se sha -lom   sha - lom a - lé - nu v'- al kol Yis - ra - él

D.S.al Fine

O-se sha-lom bim-ro-mav
Hu ya-a-se sha-lom a-lé-nu
V'-al kol Yis-ra-él v'-im-ru a-mén

עֹשֶׂה שָׁלוֹם בִּמְרוֹמָיו
הוּא יַעֲשֶׂה שָׁלוֹם עָלֵינוּ
וְעַל כָּל יִשְׂרָאֵל וְאִמְרוּ אָמֵן

May He who makes peace in the high places make peace for Israel and
for all mankind and say Amen.

DODI LI

Music: N. Chen
Lyrics: Song of Songs
Piano Arr: E. Kalendar

u - ri   tsa - fon   u - vo - i té - man

Refrain
Do-di lo va-a-ni lo ha-ro-e ba-sho-sha-nim

Mi zot o-la min ha-mid-bar
Mi zot o-la
M'-ku-te-ret mor u-l'vo-na   *Refrain*

Li-bav-ti-ni a-cho-ti ka-la
Li-bav-ti-ni ka-la   *Refrain*

U-ri tsa-fon u-vo-i té-man   *Refrain*

פזמון
דּוֹדִי לִי וַאֲנִי לוֹ הָרוֹעֶה בַּשּׁוֹשַׁנִּים

מִי זֹאת עוֹלָה מִן הַמִּדְבָּר
מִי זֹאת עוֹלָה
מְקֻטֶּרֶת מוֹר וּלְבוֹנָה (פזמון)

לִבַּבְתִּינִי אֲחוֹתִי כַּלָּה
לִבַּבְתִּינִי כַּלָּה (פזמון)

עוּרִי צָפוֹן וּבוֹאִי תֵימָן (פזמון)

My beloved is mine and I am his that feedeth among the lilies.

11

EREV BA

Music: A. Levanon
Lyrics: O. Avissar
Piano Arr: E. Kalendar

Shuv ha - é - der no - hér bim - vo - ot___ ha - kfar

v' - o - le ha - a - vak mish - vi - lé___ a - far

v' - har - chék od tse - med in - ba - lim m' - la - ve et me - shech hats - la - lim

Shuv ha-é-der no-hér bim-vo-ot hak-far
V'-o-le ha-a-vak mish-vi-lé a-far
V'-har-chék od tse-med in-ba-lim
M'-la-ve et me-shech hats-la-lim
E-rev ba

שׁוּב הָעֵדֶר נוֹהֵר בִּמְבוֹאוֹת הַכְּפָר
וְעוֹלֶה הָאָבָק מִשְׁבִלֵי עָפָר
וְהַרְחֵק עוֹד צֶמֶד עֲנָבָּלִים
מְלַוֶּה אֶת מֶשֶׁךְ הַצְלָלִים
עֶרֶב בָּא

Again the flock is flowing to the outskirts of the city and the dust rises up from the paths. Far away the bells accompany the coming of the shadows. Evening comes, evening comes.

13

Y'RUSHALAYIM

Folktune
Lyrics: A. Hameiri
Piano Arr: E. Kalendar

Text see page 77

15

LU Y'HI

Od yésh mif-ras la-van ba-o-fek עוֹד יֵשׁ מִפְרָשׂ לָבָן בָּאוֹפֶק

Mul a-nan sha-chor ka-véd מוּל עָנָן שָׁחוֹר כָּבֵד

Kol she-n'-va-késh lu y'-hi כָּל שֶׁנְּבַקֵּשׁ לוּ יְהִי

V'-im ba-cha-lo-not ha-e-rev וְאִם בַּחֲלוֹנוֹת הָעֶרֶב

Or né-rot ha-chag ro-éd אוֹר נֵרוֹת הַחַג רוֹעֵד

Kol she-n'-va-késh lu y'-hi כָּל שֶׁנְּבַקֵּשׁ לוּ יְהִי.

Refrain פזמון

Lu y'-hi a-na lu y'hi לוּ יְהִי לוּ יְהִי אָנָא לוּ יְהִי

Kol she-n'-va-késh lu y'hi כָּל שֶׁנְּבַקֵּשׁ לוּ יְהִי

A white sail facing a black cloud can be seen in the distance and through the distance the festive lights shimmer. All that we ask is "let it be."

17

AL KOL ÉLE

N. Shemer
Piano Arr: E. Kalendar

Al ha-dvash v'-al ha-o-kets al ha-mar v'-ha-ma-tok
Al bi-té-nu ha-ti-no-ket sh'-mor E-li ha-tov
Al ha-ésh ha-m'-vo-e-ret al ha-ma-yim ha-za-kim
Al ha-ish ha-shav ha-baita min ha-mer-cha-kim
Al kol é-le, al kol é-le sh'-mor na li E-li ha-tov
Al ha-dvash v'-al ha-o-kets al ha-mar v'-ha-ma-tok
Al na ta-a-kor na-tu-a al tish-kach et ha-tik-va
Ha-shi-vé-ni v'-a-shu-va el ha-a-rets ha-to-va

עַל הַדְּבַשׁ וְעַל הָעוֹקֶץ עַל הַמַּר וְהַמָּתוֹק
עַל בִּתֵּנוּ הַתִּינוֹקֶת שְׁמוֹר אֵלִי הַטּוֹב
עַל הָאֵשׁ הַמְּבוֹעֶרֶת עַל הַמַּיִם הַזַּכִּים
עַל הָאִישׁ הַשָּׁב הַבַּיְתָה מִן הַמֶּרְחַקִּים
עַל כָּל אֵלֶּה עַל כָּל אֵלֶּה שְׁמוֹר נָא לִי אֵלִי הַטּוֹב
עַל הַדְּבַשׁ וְעַל הָעוֹקֶץ עַל הַמַּר וְהַמָּתוֹק
אַל נָא תַעֲקוֹר נָטוּעַ אַל תִּשְׁכַּח אֶת הַתִּקְוָה
הֲשִׁיבֵנִי וְאָשׁוּבָה אֶל הָאָרֶץ הַטּוֹבָה

Through the sting and through the honey through the bitter and the sweet do
not destroy my hope, my yearning. Bring me back and I will return to the good
land.

19

DI GRINE KUZINE

Music: A. Schwartz
Lyrics: H. Prizant
Piano Arr: E. Kalendar

Es iz tsu mir iz ge-kum-en a ku-zi-ne	עס איז צו מיר געקומען א קוזינע
Shén vi gold iz zi ge-ven di gri-ne	שעהן ווי גאלד איז זי געווען די גרינע
Be-ke-lach vi roi-te po-me-rants-en	בעקעלאך ווי רויטע פאמעראנצען
Fi-se-lech vos be-ten zich tsum tan-tsen	פיסעלאך וואס בעטען זיך צום טאנצען

A pretty cousin came to me from Europe. Her cheeks were like red oranges, her feet just begging to dance.

PAPIROSEN

Text see page 77

DI M'ZINKE

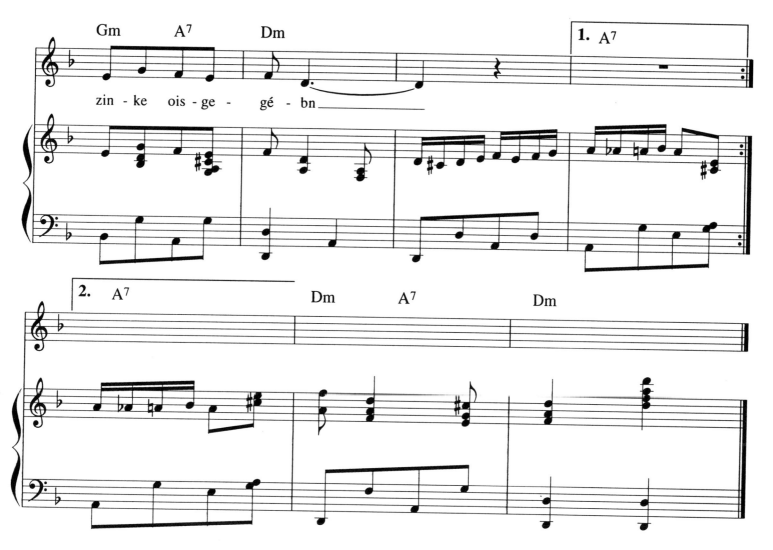

zin - ke ois-ge - gé - bn _____

He-cher be-ser
Di rod di rod macht gre-ser
Grois hot mich got ge-macht
Glik hot er mir ge-bracht
Hul-yet kin-der a gan-tse nacht
Di m'-zin-ke ois-ge-gé-bn

העכער בעסער
די ראד די ראד מאכט גרעסער
גרויס האט מיך גאט געמאכט
גליק האט ער מיר געבראכט
הוליעט קינדער א גאנצע נאכט
די מיזינקע אויסגעגעבן

Louder, livelier! Make the circle wider. God has brought me good
fortune. My youngest daughter is getting married. Dance and carry on
throughout the night.

S'BRENT

M. Gebirtig
Piano Arr: E. Kalendar

S'brent bri-der-lech s'brent	ס׳ברענט ברידעלעך ס׳ברענט
Oi und-zer o-rem shte-tl ne-bech brent	אוי אונדזער ארעם שטעטל נעבעך ברענט
Bé-ze vin-tn mkit yir-go-zun	בייזע ווינטן מיט ירגזון
Rai-sn bre-chn un tsu-blo-zn	רייסן ברעכן און צעבלאזן
Shtar-ker noch di vil-de flam-en	שטארקער נאך די ווילדע פלאמען
Alts a-rum shoin brent	אלץ ארום שוין ברענט
Un ir shtét un kukt a-zoi zich	און איר שטייט און קוקט אזוי זיך
Mit far-lég-te hent	מיט פארלייגטע הענט
Un ir shtét un kukt a-zoi zich	און איר שטייט און קוקט אזוי זיך
Und-zer shte-tl brent!	אונדזער שטעטל ברענט!

It is burning dear brothers, it is burning! Our poor little town is burning! Angry winds whip the flames. Everything is on fire! And you stand helplessly and stare while the flames grow higher and our little town burns.

SHÉN VI DI L'VONE

Music: J. Rumshinsky
Lyrics: C. Tauber
Piano Arr: E. Kalendar

28

shainst vi toi - znt zuń - en   host __ main harts ba - glikt

Dai - ne tsén - de - lach vai - se pe - re - lach   mit dai - ne shé - ne oi - gn

dai - ne chén - de - lach dai - ne he - re - lach   host mich tsu - ge - tsoi - gn

shén vi di l' - vo - ne   lich - tig vi di shte - rn   fun

29

hi - ml a ma - to. - ne   hos - tu mich tsu - ge - shikt.

Shén vi di l'-vo-ne	שיין ווי די לבנה
Lech-tig vi di shte-ren	לעכטיג ווי די שטערן
Fun hi-ml a ma-to-ne	פון הימל א מתנה
Bis-tu mir tsu-ge-shikt	ביסטו מיר צוגעשיקט
Main glik hob ich ge-vun-en	מיין גליק האב איך געוואונען
Ven ich hob dich ge-fun-en	ווען איך האב דיך געפונען
Di shainst vi toi-zent zun-en	די שיינסט ווי טויזנט זונען
Du host main hartz ba-glikt	דו האסט מיין הארץ באגליקט
Dai-ne tsén-da-lach vai-se pe-re-lach	דיינע ציינדאלעך וויסע פעראלעך
Mit dai-ne shé-ne oi-gen	מיט דיינע שיינע אויגן
Dai-ne chén-de-lech dai-ne her-a-lech	דיינע חנדעלעך דיינע העראלעך
Host mich tsu-ge-tsoi-gen	האסט מיך צוגעצויגן
Shén vi di l'-vo-ne	שיין ווי די לבנה
Lech-tig vi di shte-rn	לעכטיג ווי די שטערן
Fun hi-ml a ma-to-ne	פון הימל א מתנה
Bis-tu mir tsu-ge-shikt	ביסטו מיר צוגעשיקט

Pretty as the moon, bright as the stars, you are a heaven-sent gift to me.

BELZ

Music: A. Olshanetsky
Lyrics: J. Jacobs
Piano Arr: E. Kalendar

31

vu ch'ob ge - hat di___ shé - ne cha - loi - mos a - sach_____

Belz main shté-te-le Belz	בעלז-מיין שטעטעלע בעלז
Main hé-me-le vu ich hob	מיין היימעלע ווו איך האב
Mai-ne kinder-she yorn far-bracht	מיינע קינדערשע יארן פארברּאכט
Zait ir a mol geven in Belz,	זייט איר א מאל געווען אין
Main shté-tele Belz	בעלז-מיין שטעטעלע בעלז
In o-re-men shti-be-le	אין ארעמען שטיבעלע
Mit ale kin-der-lech dort ge-lacht	מיט אלע קינדערלעך דארט געלאכט
Yé-dn Sha-bos flég ich loi-fn	יעדן שבת פלעג איך לויפן
Dort mit der tchi-na glaich	דארט מיט דער תְחִינָה גלייך
Tsu zit-sn un-ter dem gri-nem bé-me-le	צו זיצן אונטער דעם גרינעם ביימעלע
Lé-nen bai dem taich	לייענען ביי דעם טייך
Belz main shté-te-le Belz	בעלז-מיין שטעטעלע בעלז
Main hé-me-le vu ch'-hob ge-hat	מיין היימעלע וווּ איך האב געהאט
Di shé-ne cha-lo-mes a sach	די שיינע חלומות א סך

Belz, my little town, the home where I spent my childhood years. Every Sabbath I would run down to read by the river. Belz, my little town where I had so many wonderful dreams.

33

LOS BILBILICOS

Ladino Folksong
Piano Arr: E. Kalendar

Los bilbilicos cantan	The nightingales sing
Con sospiros de amor	With sighs of love
Mi neshama mi ventura	My soul and my fate
Estan en tu poder	Are in your power

SCALERICA D'ORO

Ladino Folksong
Piano Arr: E. Kalendar

Sca - le ri - ca de o - ro de o - ro y de ___ mar - fil ___ pa - ra que su va la no - via a dar ki - du - shin ___ ve ni - mos a ver ___ ve - ni - mos a-

36

Scalerica de oro, de oro y de marfil	A ladder of gold and ivory
Para que suva la novia a dar	So our little bride can go up to take
Kidushin	Her marriage vows.
Refrain	Refrain
Venimos a ver, venimos a ver	We've come to see, we've come to see
Y gozen y logren y tengan	May they have joy and prosper
Muncho bien	And always be happy
La novia no tiene dinero	The bride has no money
Que mos tenga un mazal bueno *Refrain*	May they have good fortune Refrain
La novia no tiene contado	The bride has no riches
Que mos tenga un mazal alto *Refrain*	May they have good luck Refrain

38

KI ESHM'RA SHABAT

Oriental Folksong
Piano Arr: E. Kalendar

Ki esh-m'-ra Sha-bat	כִּי אֶשְׁמְרָה שַׁבָּת
El yish-m'-ré-ni	אֵל יִשְׁמְרֵנִי
Ot hi l'-ol-mé ad	אוֹת הִיא לְעוֹלְמֵי עַד
Bé-no u-vé-ni	בֵּינוֹ וּבֵינִי

If I safeguard the Sabbath, God will safeguard me. It is a sign forever between
Him and me.

40

DONA, DONA

Music: Sholom Secunda
Lyrics: Sheldon Secunda

On a wa - gon bound for mar - ket there's a calf with a mourn -ful eye

high a - bove __ him there's a swal - low wing- ing swift - ly __ through the sky

How the winds are laugh - ing __ they laugh with all their might

laugh and laugh the whole day through and half a sum-mer's night

Do -na do - na do - na do - na___ do -na do -na do - na don

do - na do -na do - na do - na___ do -na do -na do - na don

Text see page 78

MY ZÉDI

Megama
Piano Arr: E. Kalendar

My zé-di lived with us in my par-ent's home __ he used to laugh he put me on his knee. He spoke a-bout his life in Po-land __ he spoke __ with a bit-ter mem-o-ry __ and he spoke a-bout the sold-iers who would beat him __ they

laughed at him and tore his long black coat_____ and he spoke a-bout a syn-a-gogue that

they burned down_ and the cry-ing that was heard be-neath the smoke_____ but

zé - di made us laugh and zé - di made us sing and

zé - di made the Ki - dush Fri - day night_____ and

44

My zédi lived with us in my parents home
He used to laugh, he put me on his knee
And he spoke about his life in Poland
He spoke with a bitter memory
And he spoke about the soldiers who would beat him
They laughed at him, they tore his long black coat
And he spoke about a synagogue that they burned down
And the crying that was heard beneath the smoke
But zédi made us laugh, zédi made us sing
And Zedi made the kidush Friday night
And zédi O my zédi how I loved him so
And zédi used to teach me wrong from right.

45

L'CHI LACH

Music: Debbie Friedman
Lyrics: Debbie Friedman & Savina Teubal
Piano Arr: E. Kalendar

lach

L'chi lach, to a land that I will show you
Lech l'cha, to a place you do not know
L'chi lach, on your journey I will bless you
And you shall be a blessing, *l'chi lach*

L'chi lach, and I shall make your name great
Lech l'cha, and all shall praise your name
L'chi lach, to the place that I will show you
L*'simchat chayim l'chi lach*

SIMAN TOV

Si-man tov u-ma-zl tov
Y'hé la-nu u-l'chol Yis-ra-él

סִימָן טוֹב וּמַזָּל טוֹב
יְהֵא לָנוּ וּלְכָל יִשְׂרָאֵל

May good fortune come to us and to all Israel.

50

OD YISHAMA

Joyously

Music: S. Carlebach
Text: Liturgy
Piano Arr: E. Kalendar

51

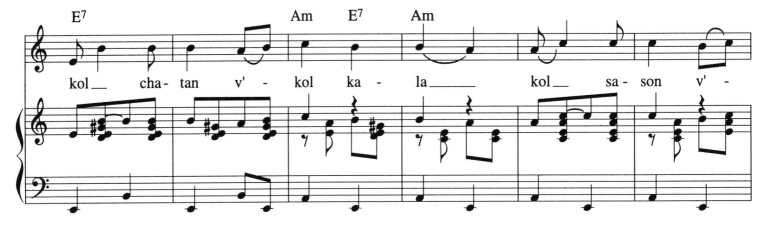

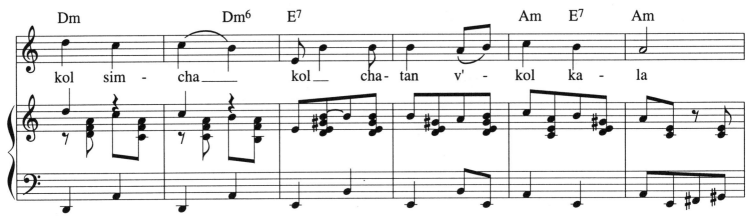

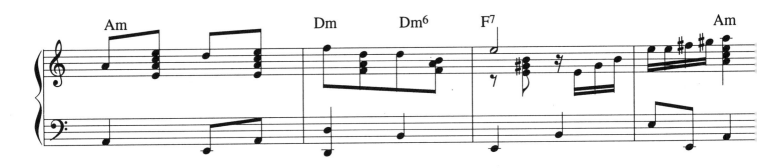

Od yi-sha-ma b'a-ré Y'hu-da
Uv'-chu-tsot Y'-ru-sha-la-yim
Kol sa-son v'-kol sim-cha
Kol cha-tan v'-kol ka-la

עוֹד יִשָּׁמַע בְּעָרֵי יְהוּדָה
וּבְחוּצוֹת יְרוּשָׁלַיִם
קוֹל שָׂשׂוֹן וְקוֹל שִׂמְחָה
קוֹל חָתָן וְקוֹל כַּלָּה

Again may there be heard in the cities of Judah and the streets of Jerusalem the
voice of gladness, the voice of bridegroom and bride.

V'HA'ÉR ÉNÉNU

Music: S. Carlebach
Text: Liturgy
Piano Arr: E. Kalendar

V'-ha-ér é-né-nu b'-to-ra-te-cha
V'-da-bék li-bé-nu b'-mits-vo-te-cha
V'-ya-chéd l'-va-vé-nu l'-a-ha-va
U-l'-yir-a et sh'-me-cha
She-lo né-vosh v'-lo ni-ka-lém
V'-lo ni-ka-shél l'-o-lam va-ed

וְהָאֵר עֵינֵינוּ בְּתוֹרָתֶךָ
וְדַבֵּק לִבֵּנוּ בְּמִצְוֹתֶיךָ
וְיַחֵד לְבָבֵנוּ לְאַהֲבָה
וּלְיִרְאָה אֶת שְׁמֶךָ
שֶׁלֹא נֵבוֹשׁ וְלֹא נִכָּלֵם
וְלֹא נִכָּשֵׁל לְעוֹלָם וָעֶד

Enlighten our eyes to your Torah; attach our heart to Your commandments.
Unite our heart to love and revere Your name so that we may never be put to shame.

Y'VARECH'CHA

Music: S.& E. Zweig
Text: Liturgy
Piano Arr: E. Kalendar

The Lord bless you from Zion; may you see the welfare of Jerusalem all the days of your life; may you live to see your children's children. Peace be upon Israel.

Y'-va-re-ch'-cha Ha-shem mi-tsi-yon
Ur'-é b'-tuv Y'-ru-sha-la-yim
Kol y'-mé cha-ye-cha
Ur'-é va-nim l'-va-ne-cha
Sha-lom al Yis-ra-él

יְבָרֶכְךָ ה' מִצִיוֹן
וּרְאֵה בְּטוּב יְרוּשָׁלַיִם
כָּל יְמֵי חַיֶּיךָ
וּרְאֵה בָנִים לְבָנֶיךָ
שָׁלוֹם עַל יִשְׂרָאֵל

56

MASHIACH

Music: M. Ben David & M. Laufer
Text: Liturgy
Piano Arr: E. Kalendar

A-ni ma-a-min be-e-mu-na sh'-lé-ma
B'-vi-at ha-ma-shi-ach
V'-af al pi she-yit-ma-mé-ha
Im kol ze a-ni ma-a-min

אֲנִי מַאֲמִין בֶּאֱמוּנָה שְׁלֵמָה
בְּבִיאַת הַמָשִׁיחַ
וְאַף עַל פִּי שֶׁיִתְמַהְמֵהַּ
עִם כָּל זֶה אֲחַכֶּה לוֹ
בְּכָל יוֹם שֶׁיָבוֹא

I believe with perfect faith in the coming of the Messiah; and although
he may tarry, I believe.

60

DAYENU

Had He only brought us out of Egypt
it would have been enough.

I-lu ho-tsi-a-nu mi-mits-ra-yim da-yé-nu

אֵלוּ הוֹצִיאָנוּ מִמִּצְרַיִם דַּיֵּנוּ

ADON OLAM

Music: U. Hitman
Text: Liturgy
Piano Arr: E. Kalendar

don o-lam a-sher ma-lach b'- te-rem kol y'-tsir niv-ra l'- ét na'-sa b'-chef-tso kol a-

zai me-lech sh'-mo nik-ra v'- a-cha-ré kich-lot ha-kol___ l'-va-do yim-loch no-ra v'-

hu ha-ya v'-hu ho-ve b'-tif-a-ra v'- hu ha-ya v'-hu ho-ve b'- tif-a-ra

Text see page 78

CHAD GADYA

Traditional
Piano Arr: E. Kalendar

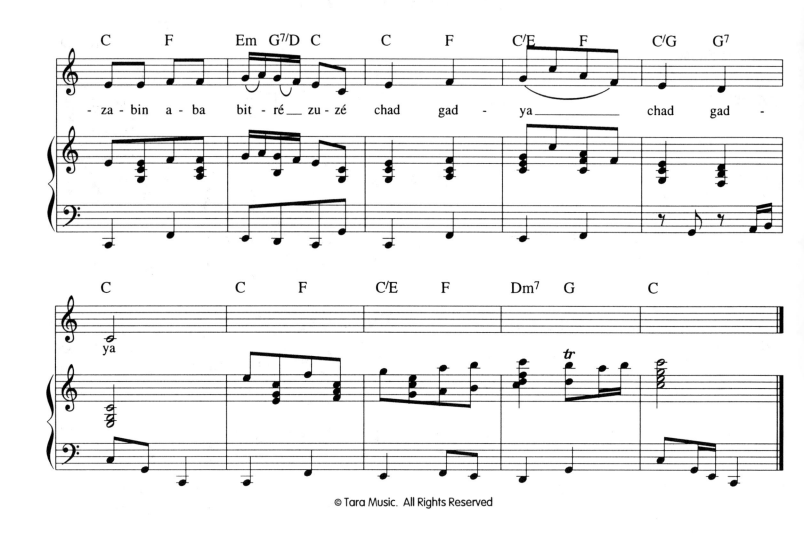

Chad gad-ya	חַד גַּדְיָא חַד גַּדְיָא
D'-za-bin a-ba bit-ré zu-zé	דְּזַבִּין אַבָּא בִּתְרֵי זוּזֵי
Chad gad-ya	חַד גַּדְיָא חַד גַּדְיָא
V'-at shun-ra v'-ach-la l'-gad-ya	וְאָתָא שׁוּנְרָא וְאָכְלָה לְגַדְיָא
D'-za-bin a-ba bit-ré zu-zé	דְּזַבִּין אַבָּא בִּתְרֵי זוּזֵי
Chad gad-ya	חַד גַּדְיָא חַד גַּדְיָא

One little goat, my father bought for two coins. Then came
a cat and ate the goat my father bought for two coins.

KOL HA'OLAM KULO

Music: B. Chait
Text: R. Nachman of Bratslav
Piano Arr: E. Kalendar

Kol ha-o-lam ku-lo ge-sher tsar m'-od
V'-ha-i-kar lo l⁴fa-chéd k'lal

כָּל הָעוֹלָם כֻּלוֹ גֶּשֶׁר צַר מְאֹד
וְהָעִיקָר לֹא לְפַחֵד כְּלָל

The entire world is a narrow bridge. But the main thing is not to fear.

SHALOM RAV

Music: J. Klepper & D. Freelander
Text: Liturgy
Piano Arr: E. Kalendar

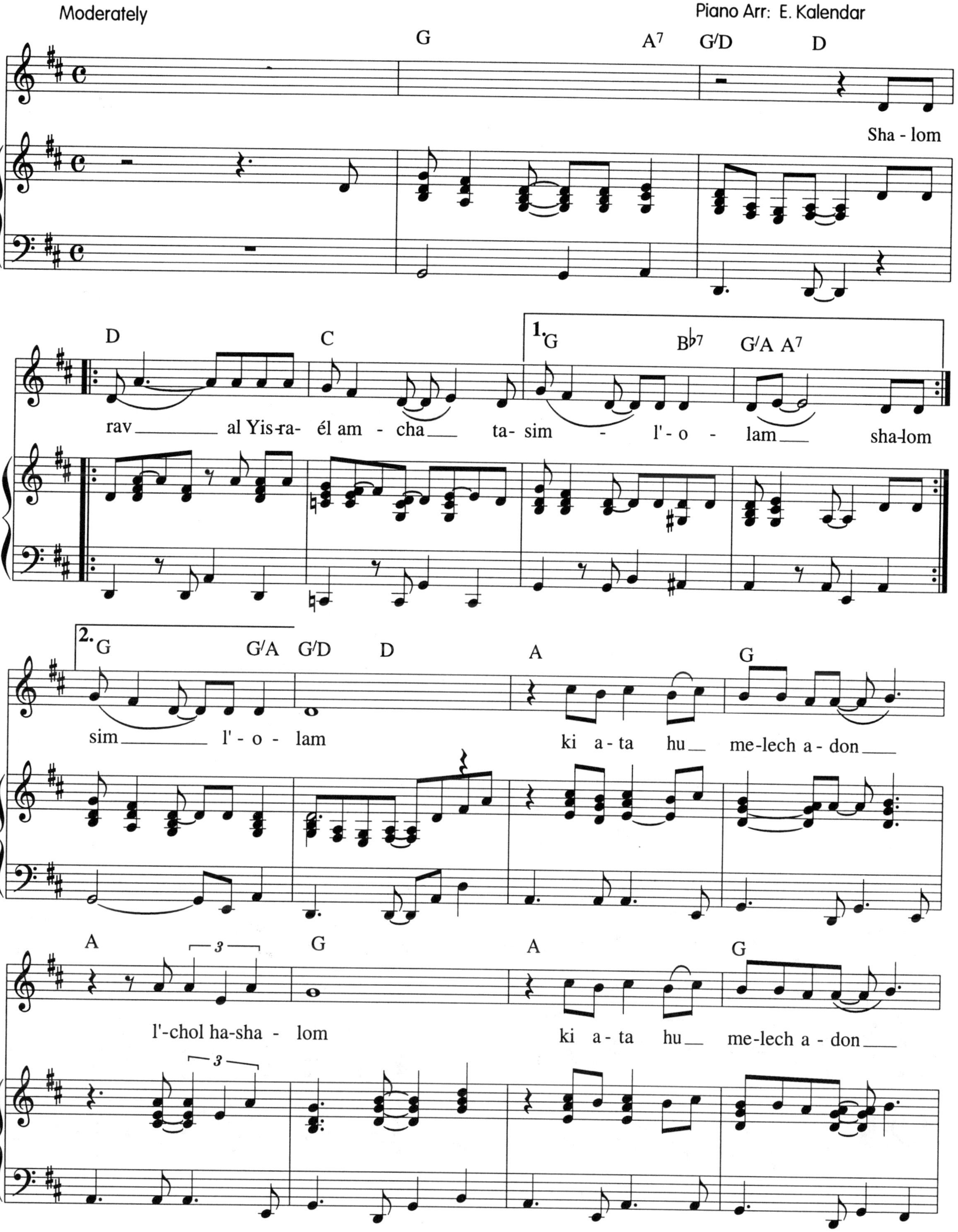
Moderately
G A7 G/D D
Sha - lom
D C 1.G B♭7 G/A A7
rav al Yis-ra- él am - cha ta- sim l'- o - lam sha-lom
2.G G/A G/D D A G
sim l' - o - lam ki a - ta hu me-lech a - don
A 3 G A G
l'-chol ha-sha - lom ki a - ta hu me-lech a - don
3

Sha-lom rav al Yis-ra-él am-cha
Ta-sim l'-o-lam
Ki a-ta hu me-lech a-don
L'chol ha-sha-lom
V'tov b'-é-ne-cha l'-va-réch
Et am-cha Yis-ra-él
B'-chol ét u-v'-chol sha-a
Bish-lo-me-cha

שָׁלוֹם רַב עַל יִשְׂרָאֵל עַמְּךָ
תָּשִׂים לְעוֹלָם
כִּי אַתָּה הוּא מֶלֶךְ אָדוֹן
לְכָל הַשָּׁלוֹם
וְטוֹב בְּעֵינֶיךָ לְבָרֵךְ
אֶת עַמְּךָ יִשְׂרָאֵל
בְּכָל עֵת וּבְכָל שָׁעָה
בִּשְׁלוֹמֶךָ

O grant abundant peace to Israel your people forever, for You are the
King and Lord of peace. May it please You to bless us and to bless all
Your people Israel with your peace at all times and at all hours.

71

SHEYIBANE BÉT HAMIKDASH

Music: I. Schorr
Text: Liturgy
Piano Arr: E. Kalendar

She-yi-ba-ne bét ha-mik-dash
Bim-hé-ra v'-ya-mé-nu
V'-tén chel-ké-nu b'to-ra-te-cha

שֶׁיִּבָּנֶה בֵּית הַמִקְדָשׁ
בִּמְהֵרָה בְיָמֵנוּ
וְתֵן חֶלְקֵנוּ בְּתוֹרָתֶךָ

May the Temple be speedily rebuilt in our days, and grant us a share in your Tora.

73

BILVAVI

Music: S. Brazil
Piano Arr: E. Kalendar

Andante with feeling

Bil - va - vi mish - kan ev - ne____ l' -ha -

dar ____ k' - vo - do ____ u - v' - mish - kan miz - bé - ach

a - sim ____ l' - kar - né ho - do ____ bil -

kar - né ho - do ____ u - l'- nér ta - mid ____